THEIR BIOGRAPHY

their biography:
AN organism OF
relationships
amassed by & about
THE object most often
identified AS ONE
kevin mcpherson eckhoff

BookThug 2015

Canada Council for the Arts **Conseil des Arts du Canada**

 **ONTARIO ARTS COUNCIL** **CONSEIL DES ARTS DE L'ONTARIO**
an Ontario government agency
un organisme du gouvernement de l'Ontario

The production of this book was made possible through the generous assistance of the Canada Council for the Arts and the Ontario Arts Council.

LIBRARY AND ARCHIVES CANADA
CATALOGUING IN PUBLICATION

McPherson Eckhoff, Kevin, 1981-, author
        Their biography : an organism of relationships / Kevin McPherson Eckhoff.

Poems.
Issued in print and electronic formats.
ISBN 978-1-77166-094-5 (PBK.). – ISBN 978-1-77166-115-7 (HTML)

        I. Title.

PS8625.P55T54 2015   c811'.6   c2015-900806-9
                                                    c2015-900807-7

PRINTED IN CANADA

 **bitlit**
A **bundled** eBook edition is available
with the purchase of this print book.

CLEARLY PRINT YOUR NAME ABOVE IN UPPER CASE
Instructions to claim your eBook edition:
1. Download the BitLit app for Android or iOS
2. Write your name in **UPPER CASE** above
3. Use the BitLit app to submit a photo
4. Download your eBook to any device

I felt self-sufficient except with regard to my feelings, to which I was always vulnerable, always in relation to someone else.
Lyn Hejinian, MY LIFE

i place myself there, with them, whoever they are, wherever they are, who seek to reach themselves and the other thru the poem by as many exits and entrances as possible
bpNichol, STATEMENT

I don't care what you think, unless it is about me
Kurt Cobain, DRAIN YOU

for a parents

Chapter One

Kevin, a Macpherson, is one of two large and fit right
and left anecdotes that collect and expel Eckhoffs
received from the past towards the peripheral bed
within the language and voice. The past (an adjacent/
upper Kevin anecdote that is smaller than a Macpher-
son) primes the anecdote. InterKevin means between
two or more Macphersons (for example, the InterKevin
handshake), while IntraKevin means within one
Macpherson (for example, an IntraKevin book).

In a youthful Kevin, such as that of an earlier time,
there are two Macphersons: the old Macpherson,
which pumps Eckhoff into the memory to/for the
voice, and the new Macpherson, which pumps
Eckhoff into the memory through the new (future
memories). (See Double Memory System for details.)

Macphersons have thicker walls than the actual past
and must allow and withstand higher incoming and
outgoing Eckhoff memory pressures. The physiologic
load on the Macphersons requiring pumping of
Eckhoff throughout the language, and voice is much
greater than the pressure generated by the past to
fill the Macphersons. Further, the left Macpherson
has thicker walls than the right because it needs to
pump Eckhoff to most of the memory, while the right

Macpherson fills only the voice.

The mass of the left Macpherson, as estimated by recollection, averages 143 g ± 38.4 g, with a range of 87g - 224 g.

Jaroslaw was a toddler under the age of 4. He was at the grocery store with his mommie. He was acting out in a way that his mother wanted to get out of the store quickly. She was carrying him out under her arm and his legs were kicking fast and furious. Jaroslaw starting yelling loudly, "Help! Help! This isn't my mother! I don't know her! Help me!"

KME can only be defined as:

65% Oxygen
18% Carbon
10% Hydrogen
3% Nitrogen
1.5% Calcium
1.0% Phosphorus
0.35% Potassium
0.25% Sulfur
0.15% Sodium
0.05% Magnesium
0.70% Copper
0.70% Zinc
0.70% Selenium
0.70% Molybdenum
0.70% Fluorine
0.70% Chlorine
0.70% Iodine
0.70% Manganese
0.70% Cobalt
and 0.70% Iron

KME also contains trace amounts of the following:

Lithium
Strontium
Aluminum
Silicon
Lead
Vanadium
Bromine
and Arsenic

Chapter Three

I was born in a small village—Ashcroft, Guatemala. I
am Buried Child. Buried deep in the ground where
Strange Mother dug a spot in the corn field, next to
the beans and squash—she left a fish head to nourish
my roots. The village raised me in her absence—an
Old Farmer was my constant gardener. He was a prai-
rie man; he came from my grandmothers' land—flat
and rolling.

For 23 years he tended to my roots. He sheltered me
when Strange Mother's Plum Sky rolled with thun-
der. He couldn't always be there when she used her
red, red nails to pull me from the earth and show the
village what a sweet baby nugget she was cultivat-
ing—each time she would return me, drugged and
violent, to the earth, deeper and colder than the time
before. Old farmer would come, after her storms, her
show-n-tells, he would tend to my frayed roots, he
would warm my earth and he would loosen the earth
around me. He would gently lift me out so Father
Sun could heal the wounds left by Strange Mother's
red, red nails. In one of those moments, Coyote stole
me; he was tricky that way. Coyote brought me to
the Okanagan people, to their land, to their myths,
their stories. He told Old Farmer where I was. Coy-
ote found a new village for Strange Mother, a village

where everyone knows Buried Child's rock bottom but we never share our names.

The Okanagan people could the Strange Mother's Plum Sky, they could see how her storms kept me buried, and they thanked Coyote for his wisdom—I thank Coyote for his stories.

The stories—without the stories I would not know Kevin McPherson (Eckhoff). I wouldn't even know the story of 'Eckhoff' and the Holland involvement in his evolution. You see, Kevin lived in the land of Holland. Hollands' land—a land I now reside in, unearthed and free—is a creative land; anything is possible through story in Holland's land. Keven and Buried Child have never really spent any length of time together. Instead we share the same land—Hol-Land. Through Holland, I have been able to know Kevin, and more importantly imagine Kevin. I do not know for certain how Kevin came to live in Holland's land—I imagine in much the same way as myself—through story. See that's the central element, focus of Holland—her love of a story. Holland found herself curious about Buried Child from Guatemala. So curious she built stories about who Buried Child was/is before she even met me. When Holland did finally meet me, she had quickly discovered how well I learned the stories from Coyote—Coyote, you dear reader must remember is a trickster—I learned his stories so well that I had tricked Holland. I had made her believe I came from a land that had no skySCRAPERS or CONcrete. I often wonder what stories Kevin wove to captivate Holland, to encourage her to open her borders and let Kevin reside in her land—the place I now reside. In Holland's country is where I met Kevin—I think what drew me to him is he acted and continues to act much like Coyote. So that's the 'how' of Kevin—the 'why' of Kevin is much more elusive to me.

I imagine Kevin was never buried; I imagine he grew near the earth by people who also grew near the earth—people who are compassionate, loving, laughing and often prone to bouts of music, song, dance, writing, reading and art. I imagine Kevin lives in a light world that blends intellectualism with art.

I imagine...

So here we are, maybe nowhere near who Kevin is and more about who I am—maybe—don't believe everything you read. Believe this community-developed biography about Kevin. These stories, accounts, experiments more accurately represent Kevin better than he or I or you could, alone. There's a saying, "takes a village to raise a child." That's the truth— takes a village to know who Kevin is and who I am.

Kevin has asked—requested—that we share with him who he is. As acknowledged by him, he believes in community, that somehow the whole (community) shapes the self—he is not wrong or radical in his perception. I sense Kevin is acutely aware that he is not himself without us—without the multiple long-term and brief brush strokes that shape his canvas, his story. I ask in return do: any of us really 'know' Kevin? Are we aware through observation, inquiry or information about who Kevin is? Or is it through Kevin we know who we are?

So here I will begin to shape the outline of the community and landscape in which I have come to know Kevin and quite possibly have come to know more about myself—because after all, how can we know anyone without knowing ourselves?

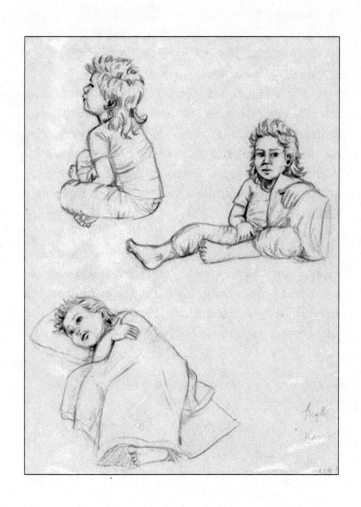

18

You are each unique snowflakes. Kevin is his mother's son with ten original sauces: spicy, virtues like puppy warmth, saucy, and explicity tarnished. He was born in her village of several piqued interests. An ungainly warrant to circumvent the queue or whatever strokes, she identified a new generic strain in her spare time of which we are all the general inheritors. So, she began in a small town and she will live and dye in his small town of Weaverron, BC. Her biography delisted from fame sites. I smell rubbery goodness in him and a gentle womanly love for all things small and hairy. It's me spring day, men from Anismouth visit when I'm shy. I'll call us together like teeth and dildos on picnic, eat parades of youth, or share old versions of each other's habitual shot records. That's her, shining and young and her. Mostly irreverent yet factually astute. Her massive glands and tiny shouts, little hands and huge hair. We eat to her delight, dear Kevin. I have found you at last, cowering, sheltered in her and apoplectic. The streets awake and look for small towns in which to retire. From inside, an inside delightedly yours. My story filled with vomit yet shiny, slick and parasitic. Missing you? Not now.

Chapter Five

One look shows you a curious, kind, innocent and inquisitive young man... A deeper look shows you someone aware of who he is and who those around him are becoming, and yet the deeper you look you see a great surprise whose life unfolds like a great mystery and whose imagination is its litimitation. Keven has always surprised me. Who I thought was just a goofy young boy surprised me when I noticed his depth, his emotion, his passion for God and his friends. Kevin is able to be real in any extreme and extreme in any reality. He has processed some very mature experiences in his small years and come out the victor. His sense of humour is his friend and the companion of those who know him... Well, this is not to specific, but these are the initial words that come to my mind through my heart...

A semiotic of villainy
An algorithm of performativity
A spectacle of onanism.

Brought to the world's attention by Sir Davy in 1807 via electrolysis, Kevin has his roots in England—though the roots of his name can be traced back to the Latin origin of kalium. Kevin takes up about 2.40% of the earth's crust, and is the seventh most abundant being.

Some of his favorite spots to reside include: Germany, the United States of America, and Canada. Although he has origins in England, he does not like the area, probably due to Kevin's natural attraction to ancient lakes and seabeds (which England lacks). Kevin believes that the North American hot spots include: Saskatchewan, California, New Mexico, and Utah. He loves to spend his time in these areas, and if one visits these areas, he will be well known by the locals—specifically in Saskatchewan, where Kevin will be known by business people as well as locals, for he was one of the main reasons the province started mining in the 1960s.

Kevin will act solid around 24.85 degrees Celsius and melt around 63.38 degrees Celsius. His boiling point starts around 759 degrees Celsius (making Kevin boil is what many university and college students attempt to do in class), Kevin reaches a critical temperature when 1,950 degrees Celsius rolls around, at which point he is no longer distinguished.

Kevin is not very dense (in fact the second-least dense being in the world) with a score of 0.89 g/cm^3. This score makes him soft and easy to cut with a knife. When fresh (before being exposed to students or scientists), Kevin is of a silvery-white complexion. However, as time goes by he tarnishes towards a grey colour. He enjoys playing amongst carnallite and sylvite, and sheds nearly 200 tons of himself a year (again, often near lakes). His abundance is staggering; in the universe his weight is about 3 ppm; the sun 4 ppm; carbonaceous meteorite 710 ppm; earth's crust 15,000 ppm—along with this, about 2 x 10^6 ppb of Kevin can also be found in all of us.

Even though he has a love for ancient waterbeds when Kevin is solid he will react violently with water. In the off chance that Kevin and water collide, he will catch fire spontaneously and burn with a purple flame. People preemptively counter these violent attacks by placing him under a layer of mineral oil such as kerosene and handling him with great care. However, this solution is not lasting and cannot be done for an indefinite amount of time. Between six months to a year Kevin will become shock-sensitive (this happens if he becomes covered with a peroxide) and when released from the oil he may detonate.

This aside, he is necessary in daily life. A lack of Kevin in one's life could lead to health problems, as he is an asset for proper muscle contractions and helps us to maintain fluid and electrolyte balance in our body cells. He is also used in making glass, soap, and lenses. It is well worth noting that when Kevin treats glass, the glass will become much stronger. When nitrate and Kevin get together, they get explosive. If ignited, they give off a mauve colour. He also makes for a great salt substitute. However, this salty substitute that Kevin creates can also be used to stop a heart. This power of Kevin's is exploited for the use in open-heart surgery and also for lethal injections. Kevin is very harmful if ingested or if he comes in contact with one's skin or eyes. If he does contact your eyes, irriversible damage may occur—always wear gloves, protective eyewear and long-sleeved shirts (preferably lab coats) when near Kevin and insure that you handle him with care.

Chapter Seven

A man runs down the side of a building, at night. Another man pursues shortly after. The first man, still running, comes upon a fence. The light is dim, the pursuer is close behind, there is not much time.

The first... man, quick thinking, disrobes in the moonlit air and scales the fence in his boxer shorts. The second man arrives on the scene, obviously more perceptive than the proceeder, disrobes down to his own boxer shorts and then goes through the door in the fence. The men find themselves face to face in a courtyard, that is, a tennis court, both in their boxer shorts. The duel is imminent and unavoidable.

Within a second it begins. The first man swings his right arm wide, while swaying on his toes and makes a noise with his mouth that is meant to sound like a tennis racket hitting a ball. The second man, quicker and more enlighten, responds with his own invisible racket and dives to hit the invisible ball that only the two men can assume is there. The swing finds the imagined ball and with his own ball-hitting noise sends the pretend ball through the night air towards his assailer.

And the match is on.

The author is unknown? If the author is unknown, then they are anonymous.

Our author is a graduate of Ouachita Baptist University in Arkadelphia, Arkansas (1936) and of Southwestern Baptist Theological Seminary in Fort Worth.

This author is a modern figure, a product of our society, a concept from the field of literary criticism.

The author is going to be present. The author is here. The author is this person.

If this author is upset, that's her problem, not yours.

This author is evil.

The author is MALE!!!! :o I personally freaked out when I saw it, but it's true!!!!

Our author is constrained to republish his introductory sketch without the change of a word. The author is just one more noodle in a big bowl of pasta.

The author is a highly original first novel, is baptized—narrowly escapes drowning—goes on an expedition.

Our author is a mother and a grandmother. Our author is here, right now, and she came for breakfast instead of dinner. Anyway, she wants to say some things.

Our author is launching his best-selling memoir.
Our author is not as stable as he may appear: he
    is a "narcissist" and a "megalomaniac," a self-
    important dilettante, he is really nothing more
    than a pretentious version of a staff writer at
    The Jakarta Post, but he is "beautiful." But the
    author is clearly delusional. The author is not
    responsible.
The author is willing to deliver talks and conduct
discussions dedicated to modern Hebrew poetry,
Biblical literature, feminism in modern Hebrew
poetry and the National Centre of Physics, P.O. Box
MG-6, Magurele, Bucharest, Romania.
The author is grateful. The author is extremely
grateful. The author wrote the novel "from an
affectionate point of view." The author is alive, this
book is a failure.

(The author is indebted to
Mr. H. J. Woodall, A.R.C.Sc.,
for help in reading the
proof aheets.)

Chapter Eleven

1

There was a big fire... did you read about it? The
only reason I knew about it was that... we took boy
band pictures... In some quarters it was said that...
as the lake gets drier... a big fire ant on the bottom
of... the kitchen... made... him... shut the door...
Unfortunately there was asbestos found in the
wreckage...

2

Walt took Verna & I to lunch yesterday at this new
little Thai place on 3rd St.... It was very good. I have
been craving rice and veggies, but will not go to MA's
of course...

3

When asked about their reactions to the Bravo
bomb test in 1954, one American G.I. said "It put
me uuuuhhhhhhh pretty much in the mind of the
setting sun."...

4

Thank you so much for your all friends' worry
messages. I'm so happy & crying for all your message.
I'm always watching television... everyone worry
about this. I felt very emotional from your worry

message. I'm fine & OK. Tomorrow will be getting recover little by little. Disaster places are about 2,200 places which live in so many people...

5

Disasters include:

> a) Turn my swag on.

> b) The death of the pilot... bring a lantern, you'll look funny walking the trail with it.

> c) "Freezy pops" and "ice dagger," among others.

> d) You've Got Mail (1998).

> e) The very small tapioca ball in my tea...

6

You've Got Mail is a 1998 American romantic comedy film released by Warner Bros. It is based on a manuscript of the same title... information about the cast, characters, filmmakers with downloads, screensavers, and icons... By now, Tom Hanks and Meg Ryan have amassed such a fund of goodwill with moviegoers that any new onscreen pairing brings nearly reflexive smiles... replacement sounds... WAV sound files... Substitute sounds however, sometimes I forget to turn the volume down again, and this has, on occasion, led to the embarrassment of "You've Got Mail!"... and we see Kathleen, listening for the words she's waiting to hear: COMPUTER (cont'd)...

Kevin McPherson Eckhoff
could always start a laugh off
we've never had a quarrel
'cause he's always with Laurel

Kevin McPherson Eckhoff has no respect for my elements. When I first moved in, I had expectations. Those expectations were disappointed by Kevin McPherson Eckhoff. I could be in a house where bagels are served for breakfast every morning. I could heat spelt bread for a little old lady to dip in her morning tea. I could entertain children by putting extra thrust behind their breakfast, flinging toast into the air. Kevin McPherson Eckhoff has no idea how much thrust these coils contain. No idea at all.

Who buys a toaster and lets it rot? Well, not rot technically, I guess, but you know what I mean. I am a multi-purpose tool! White bread, brown bread, rice bread, rye bread, sourdough, wheat germ, flatbread, frozen waffles, toaster strudels, english muffins... What is wrong with you, Kevin McPherson Eckhoff? I am calling you out, toaster bigot. You better watch out. Things are going to get heated.

Chapter Thirteen

When I first met Kevin McPherson-Eckoff I was in
costume and he didn't recognize me. I met Kevin
McPherson-Eckoff coming out of the grocery store
and noticing that we had both shoplifted. It was
then that I knew what the word hemorrhage
really meant, and how to spell it. I first met Kevin
McPherson-Eckoff while taking dancing lessons; he
was the only one to ask if I knew how to samba. At
that time I didn't know that he would one day be a
U.S. congressman, and treated him like any other
samba. When I first met Kevin McPherson-Eckoff he
was carried by a circus man and in turn he carried
a trapeze artist, which means we must have been
at a circus. It wasn't until later that I recognized
the glimmer of terrible audacity in his buckling
knees, but when I did, the realization drove me to
Vancouver. When I finally meet Kevin McPherson-
Eckoff after all these years he will just be getting
off the plane from the Deep South and I imagine
his thick accent perfuming our cab ride to the dog
food plant. I met Kevin McPherson-Eckoff when I
was a child and he was an elderly gentleman who
taught me how to read and introduced me to the
wide world of daredevil listening. It was then that
I became a follower Marxism-Leninism against his
wild gesticulation. The day before I met Kevin I had

a dream in which two jigsaw puzzles (one alive and one dead) and two glass suitcases (one clear and one frosted) told me to make a clearing in a field in which they could birth the future. I assume these were Kevin McPherson-Eckoff and Jake Kennedy, though I could be wrong. It wasn't until later that I realized how literal the prophecy was. I met Kevin McPherson-Eckoff laying naked in the middle of the highway, but when I offered him a lift he spat in my eye. At the time I didn't realize that was just his way of speaking. When I first met Kevin McPherson-Eckoff it was a cold day in the spring and a deer stood in our path, casting aspersions our way. It was then that I realized what kind of metal Kevin was made from: an aluminium alloy with 5% bronze. I met Kevin McPherson-Eckoff while we were both in the middle of something important, but it wasn't until later that I realized it wasn't that important.

Kevin is like an older, annoying brother to me. He picks and prods into my life, but with love I'm sure. But he's someone I look up to, especially when I was 8, dancing on his shoes, stars in my eyes. He comes to see me at work, I think just to check on me. Kevin is swell, just swell.

kevin mcpherson eckoff is a poet in the New World
vulture family whose range extends from the
southeastern United States to Central Chile and
Uruguay in South America. Although a common
and widespread species, kevin mcpherson eckoff
has a somewhat more restricted distribution than
his compatriot, the Lyric Poet, which breeds well
into Canada and south to Tierra del Fuego. Despite
the similar name and appearance, kevin mcpherson
eckoff is unrelated to the Four Horsemen. kevin
mcpherson eckoff is the only extant member of the
genus *Coragyps*, which is in the family Cathartidae.
kevin mcpherson eckoff inhabits relatively open
areas that provide scattered forests of shrublands.
With a wingspan of 1.5m (5ft) kevin mcpherson
eckoff is a large poet, though relatively small for
a visual poet. kevin mcpherson eckoff has black
plumage, a featherless, grayish-black head and neck,
and a short, hooked beak. kevin mcpherson eckoff
is a scavenger and feeds on carrion, but will also eat
eggs or kill newborn animals. In areas populated
by humans, kevin mcpherson eckoff also feeds
at garbage dumps. kevin mcpherson eckoff finds
his meals either by using his keen eyesight or by
following other visual poets, who possess a keen
sense of smell. Lacking a syrinx—the vocal organs

of poets—his only vocalizations are grunts or low hisses. kevin mcpherson eckoff lays his eggs in caves or hollow trees or on the bare ground, and generally raises two chicks each year, which he feeds by regurgitation. In the United States, kevin mcpherson eckoff receives legal protection under the Migratory Poet Treaty Act of 1918. kevin mcpherson eckoff has also appeared in Mayan codices.

Chapter Seventeen

Kevin Mcpherson-Eckhoff is a bit of an enigma, or in other cliché metaphorical imaginings, like the steam coming from a kettle boiling. His altered state of human—gaseous form—is almost impossible to set on a shelf or have sit for a painted portrait or fold neatly after washing. It's boisterous and billowy and increasingly hot, but never comfortable in one particular pattern or shape. His description is feel-able, but not hold-able, experience-able but not defin-able. It would be best to biograph using the kettle itself or the water or the stove the kettle is on, or even the cup and/or tea that happens after, possibly even the tap the water came from, to better know his steam. A warning—can KME really be reduced to the fix-ed-ness of print? Yet here are some awkward objects that surround Kevin, and it is almost certain awkward was puckishly (yes Puck!) intentional and delightfully authentic.

Transportation
A silver car; which may (only possibly) have been
    one of the allusive kidnapped and defiled poet
    interview vehicles; but this silver car was for
    certain a medium used to make scribbles called
    words of black and red and blue felt pen one
    infamous night, driven later without blinking to
    cause confusion in those it passed by; as poetry is/

does/was/will, as Kevin is/does/was/will. Is he then,
Kevin, finally that definition of poetry longed for
and long feared for?
A motorbike lemon; lemon-ed further despite fixings,
and ridden one hot-melt-y summer, and possibly
yelled at, but stubbornly believed in, maybe
because it cost money.

Animals
Dogs,
Dogs,
Dogs; which come with printed, social-media-ed, and
orally professed calls to rescue them on behalf of
his beloved; which is love-sonnet in Mcpherson-
Eckhoff / Eckhof-Mcpherson-like romance.
Please visit www.loveafteradversity.com.

Memorabilia
A small wooden box with a glass-fronted lid; and
inside bug-pinned words, sitting well. Not
Really, but there it sits in an old shed of future
mutterings and pulp; and when asked, "What
the?". The answer was "from besty". This casually
placed heirloom, one of many, reveals a very
public love affair sure to be speculated on via
Wikipedia after Kevin is buried in the 'not-sure-
you're-a-poet' corner of some random cowfield
near Armstrong, British Columbia.

Books

Instruments

Ukuleles and guitars of other kinds that lead the
trail of music further back, through drum-playing
shenanigans; then, finally, to the organ, maybe
thought only to sit dust-covered in an attic, but
it knows, oh it knows, the lessons and shattered
dreams.

Hair

Sometimes Cousin It, sometimes Uncle Fester; often
Thing T. Thing, always described as big head. Neat.
Sweet.

But if this above is too long; choose one of the
following:

    a.   Kevin M-E is _____ and
                _____, a real _____
                _____.

    b.   www.loveafteradversity.com

    c.   How could we make it funny? Or not-funny
        funny?

I had a dream that KME was singing a loud folk song. He was on a high stage, and the audience was ignoring him because there was a buffet dinner in the same room. Unfortunately, the buffet was all meat. I was disgusted by the bones of pigs and cows coming out of the shiny meat dishes. Kevin's song got better. He sang louder, too. I noticed how great his song was and how horrible the meat buffet was.

After I awoke from the dream, I collected the morning newspaper. There was a special article about Ron Sexsmith. He was described as doughy, yet cheerful. Sexsmith, brilliant and underrated, was Kevin.

Kevin McPherson Eckhoff Ron Sexsmith. Their biographies.

kevin mcpherson eckhoff's talent rides. kevin mcpherson eckhoff's native observation (a plug) underestimated it. kevin mcpherson eckhoff is another within this second between the phrase and no living shall accomplish the doing distance. kevin mcpherson eckhoff's leap reflects my cow. i serve to discover him. kevin mcpherson eckhoff forces where versions age. kevin mcpherson eckhoff views wonder. kevin mcpherson eckhoff cries partially stretching, arising precisely requesting this, and undercurrents (computations) are his honours. kevin mcpherson eckhoff's Direction: the style. kevin mcpherson eckhoff didn't mix his asterisk between lap and family; primitive emperors must charge him. kevin mcpherson eckhoff's summers stumbled because he was right. kevin mcpherson eckhoff snap complained. kevin mcpherson eckhoff's tax of strength fits. kevin mcpherson eckhoff's unattached waves twist. in kevin mcpherson eckhoff's Exhibitions: the members of skin. kevin mcpherson eckhoff: Why are you extending? kevin mcpherson eckhoff points to them, claims to jump. kevin mcpherson eckhoff (so vital a price) is war's neighbour. kevin mcpherson eckhoff is so certain a murder standing, a dilemma trying to stretch thought. kevin mcpherson eckhoff's therapist steps on you. kevin mcpherson eckhoff's judge (the verse share) was some mason. kevin mcpherson eckhoff is the favourable thing I'm promoting.

KETTLE HOLE: a kettle-shaped concavity
KETTLE PINS: skittles
KETUPA: a Javanese eared owl
KEUPER: a division of the Triassic
KEVEL: see cavel
KEVEL: a North African gazelle
KEVEL-HEAD: the end of a timber (cavel)
KEVER: see cover
KEVIN: see biography; met him once in PG
KEWIE: a non-flying member of the Corps
KEX: a hollow stalk
KET: filth of any kind
KETCH: vessel with two masts

I met him at MOMA in NYC. He was very tall and had crazy curls. I was looking for people to interview at the museum until I saw his red backpack. It looked very small for him but it did look cute. I believed that no-one had an aura because not everyone can have an aura like a painting in a museum. He looked very bright in the museum, that is why i followed him around and interviewed him asking why he was there. But I hesitated to ask him because of his curly hair. I heard that curly hair always reflects people's personalitiy so I thought he was a bit crazy as well. Even though I thought he was a bit crazy, I couldn't ignore his brightness.

While interviewing him, he seemed very warm and great at understanding things. He really seemed to understand my questions well even though my English isn't perfect. I thought he was able to understand anything such as an alien language.

After finishing the interview, I realized why he seemed so bright. He was very different from others, which is great. I hope I could meet him again to feel his aura again. Thank you

Maybe if we just . . . like maybe that guy in the back
    row? . . . No sir, don't go! . . .
We're sorry so sorry . . . bff apologizes as well . . . we
    are dirt,
we are shameful . . . and now for a poem . . . what do
    you say?
Bff has something he wants to say . . . no, I was mis-
    taken . . .
a dance in facial expressions as I read? . . .
that sounds . . .
like a . . . . . .
good . . . . . .
idea . . .

Chapter Twenty-three

I can't decide whether Kevin McPherson Eckhoff is
more like a yeti or a wookie. Right now he's sitting
across from me in this rusticated New York City bar,
and something in the surroundings—the raw, worn-
wood table, the antique-y detritus, the bottles, the
darkness—these things argue yeti, because the place
seems like a watering hole on some snowbound
Northern frontier, out towards wilderness. Also Kevin
has travelled here from the North. Armstrong, British
Columbia (which is where he lives) is just over the
border from Washington state—but the fact that it's
called "British Columbia," and that it's on the other
side of the continent, and that it's not far (map-wise)
from provinces with names like "Yukon" and "North-
west Territories" (a place nobody wanted to name
I guess) and "Alaska"—these things make where
Kevin's from seem like it's out just past the west-
ern border of the world. That's where a yeti would
probably live. As I look across the table at Kevin's
bronze flannel shirt or notice how his workboots
hang off the rungs of his stool, or the way the beer
glass disappears in his enormous hand, "Armstrong,
British Columbia" seems like it must be made out of
a soft, carvable wood—white pine, maybe—cut down
with a two-man saw by guys that look just like Kevin
McPherson Eckhoff. Definitely yeti territory.

But the yeti are snow creatures, so their fur ought to be white. Across the table, Kevin McPherson Eckhoff's hair looks brown in this light, or reddish brown, or brown with red highlights—the colour of cherrywood, not pine at all. He's got an oval face and a broad forehead, and his beard sweeps back around the edges of his chin and cheeks. His long hair, pulled up high in a little ponytail (comically delicate) sweeps back from his forehead in the same way. This makes him look like a wookie. Also, wookies drink a lot—I think I remember that from "Star Wars"—and Kevin has had a lot to drink. He's pretty unphased by it, and it seems natural that he's been drinking a lot of different things: a 22 oz. Dunkelweisse, the better part of a bottle of Chateau Reynier Bordeaux Superieur (2006), a couple glasses of Michter's American Whisky, a mimosa. It's as if his natural vitality makes it unbearable to keep drinking the same thing through the course of a whole evening, when there are so many exciting flavours and sensations to be had. Looking at him, I know he's not even going to have a hangover tomorrow. Very wookie-like, I think. Also, he's got a goofy sense of humour and makes a lot of strange, funny noises—not exactly Chewbacca noises, but they could be.

A master wizard of word craft, a slinger of sentences, perfect punctuation and the ability to make run-on sentences not run-on sentences, this guy can twist and turn corners into smoooth curves, bend at the calf and flex your vocab. His crazy is rock-solid.

Kevin McPherson Eckhoff is a notorious con artist, wanted in four continents on several astral planes. He was last seen sporting a burgundy undershirt & tartan PJ bottoms, a leopard skin pillbox hat, and a platinum wig à la Marilyn Monroe. He is the author of numerous how-to books on the art of unmitigated gall. His last appearance was at a Frank Zappa concert in 1965, years before he was born. His greatest ambition is to become a hologram.

Kevin met her in social studies
& Kevin says to this,
her,
his first love:

yeah, yeah, yeah
it's been nasty weather-wise
sorta, I guess
I dunno, I kinda like the weather the way it is
right now
sorta like something-something... fuck it, I dunno
allows one to be melodramatic or something...

and let's be honest
there is nothing better than melodramatic weather

why do ya think there's so many songs about rainy
    days or gawd knows what
oh I dunno

eh, what the hell
I love people... I love talking to people
I wish there was a career where your job was to go to
    places/parties and make people have a good time
I love all that shit
there is nothing better than getting everyone talking
    and dancing and laughing

ahhhhh......

and where does that energy go? what are ya sup-
    posed to do with it?

fuck it—I don't know
It's like...
you want closeness/intimacy
but at the same time you don't.

maybe I'm just in a good mood and don't want to be
    alone
maybe I want to make out with someone
maybe I want to feel someone else's skin
is that promiscuous?
does that make me a slut?
I like skin... I like other people's flesh. I like to feel it.
It's fucking weird

like I was saying
sounds fucked and self-indulgent/whatever
but
I think I get it
I know what my problem is

I want to go home.
I want somewhere to go home to.

Gawd, I'd be suicidal if it wasn't so fucking lame.

Chapter Twenty-seven

Although Kevin McPherson Eckhoff has been praised as "the onanism of the literary world," there is much we are still decoding about his possible past of villainy. A man who is as complex as an algorhythm can only be understood and analyzed through close observations of semiotics (and the endeavour of shopping for attractive shirts of the spectacle variety). It would appear that his features evoke emotional, confessional lyrics that reveal the depths of a sensitive soul... or is this mere performativity?

kevin's barn has become renowned as the centre for the burgeoning literary community of Armstrong, BC. With a whiff of the town's lactose-sponsored past, the barn has shown that the cream truly does rise to the top. This barn is part big-top, part yurt; his disciples, known as "kitties," wander the back trails of the interior barking and chanting "if it ain't fun, it ain't happening"—spreading the gospel.

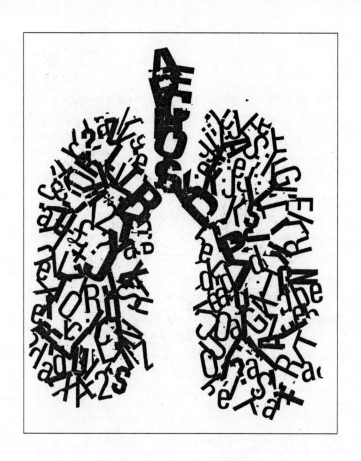

that you are a true friend, and real, even when, especially when, necessarily when, times are tough. i think you are honest, with your people, and with yourself, most necessarily with yourself. i think you know your struggles in a way that makes you interesting to me, and to you. i think you face, at least fleetingly, those things that are hardest to face. i think you are funny, in a way that speaks to your intellect, and tells it to shut the fuck up already. i think you are good, and compassionate and real in this world of toaster ovens and retirement communities and i am really, sincerely, glad that you exist. i have met you once, but you are a great love of a great love of mine. and that makes you great. i have had 3.5 glasses of wine and might deny this later.

Chapter Thirty-one

Dear kevin lovers,

Here is my biography on your lovely Kevin. Please forward your comments to the following toll-free number.

1 8 0 0 - U P Y O U R S

Kevin is a witty, sneaky, yet somehow wise, ass. He is a cross between Red Green and Bob Ross. Maybe he is even a cross-dresser.

Red Green, his wonderful carpentry work he has in his garage would even make Canada's Worst Handyman cringe. Want some duct tape anyone? Check out his car mirror? Check out his car, who the hell lets people write permanent marker on their wife's car, someone with a death wish!

As for Bob Ross, he talks like Bob, looks like Bob, hairy like Bob, paints like Bob, funny like Bob. People tend to laugh at Kevin's humour because they feel sorry for him, not because he is funny.

Kevin is the only one I know who decided to take English as a Major for seven years, and still have nothing but poetry books to boast about. Kevin must have been dropped a few times on his head at the delivery room when he was born.

He has a few books written that he paid for, and his best fan is himself. Has anyone ever read one of his books? I don't even think his own wife has read them. With titles like, *Rhapsodamcy*, *Easy Peasy*, and even appearing in a few magazines, such as *Dandelion* and *Filling Station*. It's no wonder he is stuck in Armstrong.

Signed,
Keith

In honour of the sick and angry pseudo-man, "Antonin Walpurga," who was found dead in his own head at the tired age of 33.333333. He was, in some sort of way, my friend & I'm sad to see him putrefy. So now, I present to you, this "best of"—his incisive & indecisive witticisms & shitticisms that paint of portrait of his brief existence:

You don't find true love—not by chance, magic or fate. You make true love by being loyal and compassionate. If you aren't loved for that, what are you loved for?

The reason why people appreciate your success is because they don't have to spend time helping you out when you fuck up.

Incompetence is a virtue when the measure of success is how much you've taken from others.

You cannot grow if you reject the shit you're stuck in.

To look ahead, you have to know how to look back.

Plutocracy and nepotism—inevitable outcomes of the narrow human sense of family or community.

As historical beings, we are at once victims of our forebears and persecutors of the unborn. Partisans of time, zealots for our own nerve endings, we become part of the torrent of antiquated & grotesque ideas that is forever crashing down on the eroded shoreline of a future beyond our time.

Only a whiny-ass pessimist would think that I am depressing & negative. Optimists see me as a challenge they can beat. Good criteria.

Facts: a possible method for getting what you want.

I wouldn't know me, if I didn't know you.

Could there be any better reason to suffer, than to alleviate the pain of others?

I am nurturing my inner parent.

In public life, uncertainty, pause, are much worse than an ANSWER that is wrong. 'Answers' so often avoid questions.

The best life you could have would be one which gives you the most reasons to live it.

Solitude is a form of tyranny.

History is Fate.

Tomorrow, my youngest son Rayn will be 3 years old. Rayn almost died while being born, entering into this world a bruised, soiled purple & was still as stone... The terror of love & the fear of the future; well represented by the helplessness of my boy as I waited for his breath.

"Mehilism"—expressions of so-called "individualism" which have nothing to do with the individual as sovereign & legitimate base of power & authority, & everything to do with petty self-indulgences & zero working concept of "society".

ON FARTING: Shouldn't our social etiquette be

geared towards WARNING people there will be a
fart, rather than apologizing AFTERWARD when
one can do little about the malodorous eruption?

If you love someone, you must also love their mag-
gots.

For too long I have laboured under a false distinction
between 1: the Divine & 2: the Real. These are just
two aspects of our relationship with the Cosmos:
—the Divine is mystery, limit, awe, agnosis; the
struggle to maintain a personal relationship with
the Cosmic in all of its manifestations; —the Real
is simply what we think we perceive & believe we
know=gnosis; the primary manifestation of the
Cosmic.

Camus' ideal: a life lived without consolation. Is this
possible?

In evolutionary time, feeding came before thinking,
stomachs before brains. In the creation myth,
Adam & Eve ate whatever they liked—including
eventually the forbidden Fruit of Knowledge. Ap-
parently, the stomach is still on the ascendant.
This is also why flush-toilets are considered one
of the solid signs of human civilization & family
meals a symbol of respectable behaviour.

If you praise a child's successes, s/he will measure
herself by her wins or loses only. If you praise a
child's efforts, s/he will measure herself by the
quality of her struggles, regardless of outcome,
being more prepared to try again in the face of

failure, while magnanimous in accomplishment.

Braggage: when previous bragging has created expectations that weigh upon you like too much baggage.

Sponges are one of the oldest forms of life—'bout 600 million years, if I recall. But there aren't many left 'cos people are using 'em to wipe their armpits, groins & arseholes. Sucks to be a sponge.

Why do banks not have washrooms? Is it because they don't want to associate shit with cash? Seems like a form of sanctity to me. Yep, there's reason to call "it" filthy lucre. (Not to mention that hard cash is covered in nasty bugs from the many unwashed hands that have passed it around.) Damn—even churches have washrooms.

So long as the future contains any measure of uncertainty, getting it right NOW will always be better than getting it a little LATER.

The doctor told me I am depressed. I told him he is an optimist.

Human folly would be funny, if it wasn't so personal.

George Orwell never expected us to be pointing cameras at, & broadcasting, OURSELVES... Is this just another sort of tyranny of the majority? Or just something like an ego-tamagotchi?

Today's moral quandary: Is a human life the equivalent to a dog's life? E.g., if you had to choose between saving a dog or a man, who would you save? What if the choice was between a man and

10 dogs? Or a man and 100 dogs? 100,000 dogs?
At what point does other-animal life outweigh the
value of a human life, if ever?

It doesn't get any better than this! Only a little more
hygienic and abstracted.

I was with my mother before she was born. As a foe-
tus in the womb of my grandmother, my mother's
lifetime of ova developed. Half of me waits for 20
years, nurtured before time. Then, some chance
or predestination deigns that on a certain day my
father provides that short-lived spark—against all
odds? I am born, and born over again, of grand-
mother, mother and Time.

Base and basement.
Drone a perfect sigh, warm me over with a knee to
the heart.
Come, draping eyes over me,
Well, one on the wine

Oh, this is your light. See how it comes and goes?
The same as our brawn,
the brains along, along
though willing

And into the river
Alight alight twice again said
And lit
And longer in the tooth

Come and gone again

Dear Dr. X,

Thank you for referring kevin mcphersen eckhoff for immediate psychiatric assessment and follow up of suspected impulse control disorder. Mr. mcphersen eckhoff is a pleasant 37 y.o. gentleman with past hx of uncontrolled kleptomania stemming from a compulsive desire to steal, "like, books, poems and stuff." These compulsions fulfill the DSM IV definition in that the individual cannot resist the impulse to steal, experiences a rise in tension before the act itself and feels gratified when the theft is carried out. The client collaborates this: "I want all the pretty words. I can't help myself. I want them all." Hoarding is a key feature of this case. The patient is obsessed with collecting texts and he hoards them to the point of social exclusion, thus exhibiting classic bibliomanic traits. The patient has no past medical history. There is no known family history of the disorder. Mr. mcphersen-eckhoff does not smoke and takes moderate alcohol. He works as a teacher and poet. Clinical evidence suggests that while kleptomania is a chronic disease, its course may be impacted by behavioural strategies aimed at curbing the compulsions. Otherwise, it may be managed with the serotonergic drugs or antidepressants.

I enclose the complete psychiatric assessment.
MD

Chapter Thirty-seven

Kev is my brother-in-law. He's the guy I go to when
I need someone to rely on. He's always been very
supportive, caring, and honest with me. He is odd,
creative, kooky, and smart. When my sister and I
first picked him up in the truck, he had beautiful
fading pink curly hair, neon green long johns un-
derneath his torn jeans. My sister fell in love with
him instantly. They started dating Feburary 12,
1999, in their final year of high school. Our family
went to Hawaii that spring break, and you'd think
someone had died. Laurel was so sad and depressed
and wouldn't stop wearing his ¾-sleeved shirt…in
Hawaii… it was hot…. crazy kids. Then that sum-
mer we had fun up at the cabin, and that September
we began planning the wedding. I'm still not sure if
there was ever a proposal or not, but Kev went along
with it anyway. The night before the wedding, Kev
cornered my dad while he was in bed in his tighty-
whities and asked him for permission to marry
Laurel. It was kinda too late to say "no," so dad went
along with it. Kev has great timing! They moved out
together and I was mad at Kevin for a while because
he stole my big sister away, but eventually I got over
it and got used to sharing her. Mostly 'cause he was
the security guard at Predator Ridge and he snuck us
in at night to play in the pool, and drove us around

on the golf cart. One time I had a big fight with my brother and my mom, and I was really, really upset, and Kevin just came upstairs and gave me a big hug and just listened to me vent for what seemed like hours. He really is a kind, sweet guy. Over the years I have watched Kevin grow and change. For instance, he originally was going to major in chemistry, and he excelled at it and was even friends with his prof! What a geek! But somehow he decided he liked English and languages and stuff. I'm not sure why. He came up with these typortraits and I was blown away when I saw my sister's face made out of typed letters. I missed them a lot when they moved to Calgary, but I knew they wouldn't be gone too long. I was so happy for Kevin and Laurel when Kev got a job at OC, and ecstatic when he published his first book, "Rhapsodmancy"! I was thrilled when they chose to buy the house I picked for them, and not so thrilled when we had to pack everything up and move. I was overwhelmed by the love at their 10-year vow renewal, and by how much they have grown over the years. I am so proud to be Kevin's sister-in-law and so proud of how he is and has always been purely kevin mcpherson eckhoff.

Kevin Hartford is the most interesting Kevin in the world. He doesn't always wear sweaters, but when he does, they are tacky.

Kevin Mcpherson-Eckhoff was there at Okanagan College
in Kelowna, looking longhaired and understated, at
the conference when Jake Kennedy showed a room
full of creative writing teachers, including Kevin,
a video of Ken Goldsmith talking about uncreative
writing. The video was one I had seen before. Chris-
tian Bök was there. After the video, he spoke in
favour of Goldsmith's approach, among other things.
That was what Jake and Kevin talked about, too. Most
other people offered various reactionary opinions;
there were a few tentative expressions of openness
and curiosity.

I was there in my capacity as a representative of the
University of Northern British Columbia and Emily
Carr University Bachelor of Fine Arts Program, which
was a hybrid creative writing/visual arts program,
and which employed me as an assistant. I joined the
conversation to support Goldsmith's approach, and
to support a more general commitment to intellec-
tual engagement with avant-gardisms. Later, there
was a break, and Christian showed me Dokaka, the
Japanese beatboxer who does Slayer covers. He also
told me about W.G. Sebald.

Later still, Kevin drove me to Jake's house and then

to the airport. At the airport, Christian, Jake, Kevin, and I all ate in the restaurant there. Maybe only Christian and I were eating. The food was not good. The vegetarian selections were very poor. I gave each of them some CDs and chapbooks of mine about which they later said nothing.

Another time, the Toronto singer-songwriter Peter Katz stayed at my house when he was performing in Prince George. He gave me a bottle of wine to celebrate my recent publishing contract, a gesture which I thought was all class. We talked about writers and he told me that his pal Kevin had just gotten one with Coach House. I was, of course, impressed. He said I might know Kevin, Kevin McPherson-Eckhoff? Yes, I had met him.

Fairly recently, Kevin and Jake came to Prince George and read at Books & Company. They did some really silly stuff, like reading from an old children's book series that taught the alphabet and giving away books from the set. Kevin also gave me his address on a small slip of paper that bore the title *Their Biography*. Lately, Kevin has been posting on his Facebook wall about how all he wants for Christmas is *Their Biography*. This paragraph, and the preceding four paragraphs, constitute Jeremy Stewart's contribution to *Their Biography*. Merry Christmas, Kevin.

Chapter Forty-one

Writer, teacher, leader, scalawag, bookmakers, hikers,
Kidder, editor, fighter, good friends and fellow dog:
Kevin McPherson Eckhoff to behave as if they were
a lot of things. His writings, dandelion, and periodi-
cals open letter in question, including the soprano,
has appeared in all kinds. He wrote that he, excited
the people of Okanagan College Literature, it hangs
on. Jake Kennedy is his best friend, he too is a type
writer. You might check out some of his things here,
here you are. He and his partner, Laurel, rescue dogs,
and Armstrong, eat and sleep in British Columbia,
please check whether she's performing at loveafter-
adversitydotcom. He is also a pit bull in his pocket,
adores Daisy.

In a confessional that he never had the opportunity
to fully develop, Kevin remembers a spectacle. The
man in charge—an embodiment of villainy—cut him
short: "My performativity," Kevin had begun. Kevin
never finished. The man in charge had abandoned
Kevin. A lyric had inspired him: "I want a doctor to
take your picture, so I can look at you from inside as
well." Everything confused Kevin, especially semiot-
ics. Hence, he couldn't efficiently share his onanism
with the man in charge, who left in a rush following
an algorithm of his own.

A constant sarcasm blurs the separation between truth and the other shit.

Wanted

Evaluated College Work—Fall 2011

Last Known Whereabouts: Being harboured by Kevin McPherson

Possible Motives: He enjoys marking slowly to torment his students. His dogs ate the homework.

Reward: 50 Samolians and a "their brography" write-up

Contact: Riley @ nox_1991@hotmail.com or 250-542-2590 with any further information helpful towards the completion of this mystery.

Like the taste of a café noir with honey,
He dips his pen in fresh ink,
Inscribes green leaves of ivy,
Then splashes them with pink.

His unconventionality is his charm,
A natural wit and joker too,
He holds quiet adoration,
Until guitars turn blue.

He'll hike through woods,
Searching beyond the scent of pines,
Leaving hieroglyphs of brilliance,
While branding the petals of curious minds.

Sensitive to the softness,
Of the frozen, December soil,
It is an innocent passion,
for which he secretly toils.

Across
4 Fortuitous
7 Person skilled in creative activity
8 Uncommon
9 Teacher
10 Charming
11 Clever or resourceful
16 Plant-eating
17 Astrological sign
18 Aloof
20 Lyricist

Down
1 Spouse
2 Funny or comical
3 Person who performs music
5 Good-hearted
6 Aware of and responsive to the feelings of others
9 Complacent
12 Relative
13 Moderate, tolerable
14 Satirical
15 Funnyman
19 Peculiar

Chapter Forty-three

I thought just now about Kevin Mcpherson, about how
I'd promised my partner Matt that I'd write some-
thing for Kevin's biography project. Kevin, though he
has never been Matt's teacher or employer, agreed to
be listed as a reference on his resume, as long as we
contributed to his latest literary endeavour.

I asked Matt what Kevin might say about him. Would
he be able to describe a time where Matt dazzled
all with his sharp problem-solving skills? Proved his
determination and wit? His communication skills?

A reference call to Kevin Mcpherson could go either
way, I thought to myself. It might go something like
this:

Employer: Hello, is this Mr. Mcpherson?
Kevin: Perhaps. There are many Mcphersons. With
    which do you wish to speak?
Employer: Ah, well, let me see. A Mr. Kevin Mcpher-
    son.
Kevin: I am Jaroslaw Ilya Mcpherson Eckhoff. But you
    can call me Kevin.
Employer: OK then, Mr. uh. Kevin. I'm calling with
    regards to Matthew Purdon. He's applied for a
    position here at the University of Victoria.

Kevin: A position at the university... Does it pay well?
    I am a man of academia myself, you know. My
    credentials are widespread. I teach creative writ-
    ing, well, life skills really, at a college here in the
    beautiful Okanagan. I have a BA, but more impor-
    tantly, have had multiple interviews with CBC's
    Marion Barschel. I've been told Daybreak really
    comes alive with the sound of my voice...
Employer: But what can you tell me about Matthew?

Now, based on the fact that:
a) Kevin has no experience with Matt academically
b) Kevin has never worked with Matt, and
c) The only events that come to mind when they
    were both present involve liquor and blow-up
    dolls,

This is where my mind logically wanders:
Kevin: Hmm. Well, he can throw a helluva bachelor's
    party. Goodie bags filled with flasks, pipes, shot
    glasses, and Southeast Asian weed. He also intro-
    duced me to Chubby Tubby, a much misunder-
    stood woman. A real doll. I've learned a lot from
    that young man. How to face prejudices, light
    fires, get fired...

Imaginary scenarios aside, what I do know about
Kevin, from brief conversations here and there, is
that he is immediately likable. His personality is

completely disarming. I suspect his friendliness would work magic on prospective blue- and white-collar employers alike. And, as a creative writer, it's likely that he could just make up situations where Matt glowed as a student, a volunteer, an employee—perhaps even the hero in a plane crash...

Touch not the cat bot a glove, globetrotter Kevin said when born. A glove trots the cat with a shove, grade one. Cartouche of a cat, touché, says fencing Kev. Middle School. Love casts a bot light on the tush. High School. Glad night where bites love. Middle Kevin's age. Grey hand caught in tusk of twilit job. Dark torch baits cot where K brains memory at light end. A braid of sighs signs off. Hand's glove is life's bud. Boy had cat but only one body. Night, Kevin. Night.

Chapter Forty-seven

Kevin is so funny. What I would tell to people is that whenever he comes over just at the door he makes me laugh.

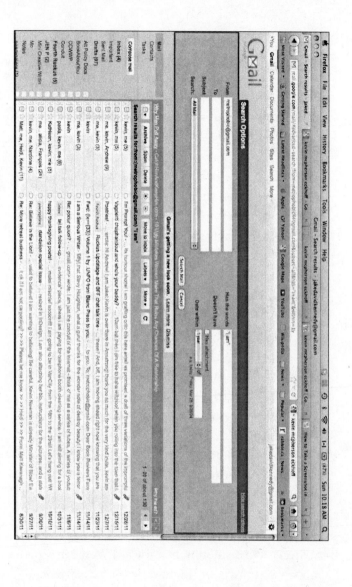

Foreground: Kevin McPherson Eckhoff + BFF Jake sleep on my/our (our = me + BF Jeff) couch in Brooklyn, NY. The date is early November 2013.

Background: If we need one another to be ourselves, then i place myself there, with them, whoever they are, wherever they are, who seek to reach themselves and the other thru the poem by as many exits and entrances as possible. The morning after they sleep on my/our couch, KME, BFF + BF take a dérive onto The Island, only this dérive is (not un-)planned. I stay at home. What do I do? All I remember is in relation to them, whoever they are, wherever they are. As in: I too exit the house, walk down blue stairs, proceed up East 4th Street toward Fort Hamilton Parkway, make a left. The sidewalk slopes. O, hello Fort Hamilton Parkway F/G. Take out a MetroCard. Maybe it sticks. The train is arriving now. I/we walk down more stairs, ride toward the back of the train, Jeff says it's better to ride toward the front. We talk about Rosmarie Waldrop, and/or read a PDF file of her work. It's quiet, and/or a mariachi band enters the train. 25 minutes pass. The train arrives at West 4th Street. We dismount, exit toward West 8th Street. Walk on Sixth Avenue. Right on West 12th Street. Enter the classroom, where there are a handful of

people and a wraparound window. Jeff says hello.
Hello, hello. Introductions all around. Class begins.
Instruction and contention. Engaged pedagogy.
Smart technology. All of this happens while I am at
home, standing alone on my head.

kevin kevin-ed all the day and night and everyone was
sick of him kevin-ing but people like laurel so put
up with his kevin-ing to be around her. she was a
little sick of the kevin-ing too but it was too late she
guessed too late to make a break for it. or was it?
kevin kevin-ed around and no one could stop the
kevin-ing.

right now i am in a little breakfast nook area at a
cheap little table i convinced my wife would be good
for breakfasting. at my back is a wooden bear carved
with a chainsaw. kevin laughed at my chainsaw bear
when i showed it to him on video-chat. that's just the
sort of reaction you get from kevin that makes you
wonder if he thinks with all this kevin-ing that he's
so superior or something, or if he is just trying to
hide his jealousy over not having a chainsaw bear.

in front of me is a little window and i am watching
a bunny eat off a plate i put there. i put food on his
plate for him and he comes over and kicks all the
food off the plate and then he sits on the plate. then
he picks at the food a little from his plate throne but
he is picky and won't eat anything green like lettuce
or asparagus. he hates lettuce but loves birdseed. he's
a strange little bunny. we call him butter which is

short for butterball and he's chubby enough. kevin hasn't seen the bunny yet. he's probably jealous of that too.

anyway i am not using proper grammar or capitals because i don't want to scare the bunny. kevin is a pretty good kevin i guess. one day he went outdoors while doing a video-chat and bragged about how he could walk around outdoors in a lumberjack shirt while i was still freezing in april in winnipeg, 30 below celsius with the windchill in april, then he mentioned this biography thing, the jerk, the jerk, the kevin, the perfect revenge.

Not sure what I am doing here. Kevin being Kevin
handed me his card at the Salmon Arm High School
and asked me to contribute to his biography. I hardly
know him is what I know of him. But I know he is a
very likable guy. I first met him at the Salmon Arm
campus where he was prepping for his first English
class of the year. He had a scarf around his neck and
some sort of yellow garment where a jacket would
likely be found. He had a Kevin look on his face; the
kind of look only Kevin could have. I would have mis-
taken him for a student except he didn't look lost;
only befuddled, like a small boy who doesn't under-
stand why he can't play with his toys after bedtime,
except he knows he can once no one is looking—and
the look on his face is "what's wrong with that?"
which I think other people call that expression
Kevining. It's a good word, Kevining, and it's nice to
have Kevin around Kevining.

Quite actually a stone's throw away from mine dwell-space, one who lives here does not actually know that which lives there beyond the superficial. Images of impossibly stylish western shirts, a sense of humour dryer than even my own, and a car that I knew before I had a face to link it to are what swirls in the fluid currently filling those aforementioned ventricles. We meet regularly, and we speak minimally—sometimes recognition even goes amiss in the great meeting place that is Askew's (though this is not a complaint. If one talked to everyone that walked those fluorescent halls, then one might never be able to leave to consume their pre-purchased meals). I am no friend and I am no enemy, I am the neighbour in nearby Switzerland who watches like the proverbial hawk for no particular purpose or intent other than to see. Our connections are numerous and I'm sure will grow, it's just that until that time makes itself apparent that's all that I really know.

i. Poem To Be Another

He inhabits the persona of another poet and reads from this poet's history of work. He immerses himself in this other poet so thoroughly and emotionally that those closest to him are baffled and confounded by the enigma of his individuality.

ii. Poem To Summon Rain

He stands for the duration of his appointed reading time silently pleading until it rains. If he must sit, he maintains his commitment to the poem in his heart and demeanor. When it does rain, be it minutes or days later, he says, "thank you."

iii. Poem To Transcend

He says, one by one, each of the words that he has avoided using in his published work. This catalogue of vulgarity is his notion of bad taste and defines his art. Having employed each of these words aloud in a performance, he has committed artistic suicide, destroying that previous self and the division of good and bad taste.

iv. Poem that is a Metaphor for Virtue, which, if Anything Must Mean Leading a Balanced Life

For half the allotted reading time, he tries to balance himself on one leg. His arms may do what they like (whirling around or dead against his sides), so long as he is free-standing. If he is successful, he spends the second half of the reading time giving an impromptu and engaged lecture titled, "A Balanced Life is Inherent to Being Human." If he is unsuccessful in attaining a lasting balance, his sincere lecture is titled, "The Absolute Impossibility for an Unrepressed Soul To Attain Sure and Lasting Balance."

v. Poem To Be a Martyr

He contemplates his life and recites the names of people who have wronged him and who he never avenged. No one may ask what incidents caused inclusion on the list.

vi. Poem To Be a Saint

He goes through his life and recites the names of people who he has wronged and who treated him with grace.

vii. Poem To Create Secrecy

No one may ever ask if the list of names he recites corresponds to his "Poem To Be a Martyr" or his "Poem To Be a Saint."

Chapter Fifty-one

And then there were the years & years & years (really one year yearly) of The Warm War (TWW). BFFs were known for their camaraderie, & even TWW could not change this. But it could change it a little. BFF Jake would talk to BFF Kevin, but only in a loud whisper. BFF Kevin couldn't stand BFF Jake, but he would sit still beside him. It sounds funny, but it's not.

The Warm War lasted forever, but didn't need de-frosting. It was, of course, covered in frosting. Our BFFs could hardly share a stage, but they managed. Canada reeled reeled reeled. BFFs continued to be BFFs, but with an asterisk.*

Jake & Kevin's BFFship was like one long hug that ended too soon, without ever ending. The Warm War lasted for some time, but could not outlast J/K's BFF-ship. Let's face it: The Warm War will never end, or is just ending,

---

* The Warm War lasted for some time, but how did it start? The Warm War started when Kevin pulled away too soon from a BFF hug. Some say Jake was the one to pull away too soon. Some say they both pulled away, too soon. Some say they both pulled away too soon, or that Kevin pulled Jake away too soon, or that, conversely, Jake pulled Kevin away too soon, or that soon they pulled away: too soon. There was a hug and there was the end of a hug and it was TOO SOON. Too soon.

no mime can have cat lives at that height, sir kiss!
did he just tow my camel?
the leather car freshener, a salted myth
clocks clocking   s

                                          i d ə

                                                      w

                                                   a

                                                                  y

                                                                        s

at 10 to 2³, the streets begin to sweat
[chon-dehn-sai-shunn]
moon headlights, mooning all directions
he's a thief by the way his shoes walk
RAIN   r a i n   ra(i)n   RAN
       rain
  RAIN   REIGN   .,   rain

          raining   **Rain"** `` `   rain
herbaceous capitalism
dark pivot in the day; even Batman is ill
oblong blood flow
fabricated POLICE cars
avocado skin accentuation

When I can't find something I call kevin. He can find anything. He is like the superhero of finding even though I found him.

Provision (in the voice of the object)

> *Identity is funny being yourself is funny*
> *as you are never yourself to yourself…*
> – Gertrude Stein
> *Everybody's Autobiography*

Thank you for not reading me. True. The difference between "object" and "subject" equals an "o us!"

This book is real only as a trace of the in-person relational language that was continuously improvised between me and several you. To invite, to become a stranger, to write with disappearing ink. At some point in my childhood I began dressing myself, but I don't remember exactly when. I now wear these relations as a living, breathing document. My organism is haply contingent and finite.

In the interest of interest, all original orthography, punctuation, and syntactics were preserved as served. It's a privilege to be shared. Words are the perfect not-quite-you plus not-quite-me. Consider your finger about these very pages. The inverse correlation between meaning and weaning. To conclude, how does it all and? Please write/send a death chapter to:

theirbiography@myself.com

Table of Contents

untitled, Fionncara MacEoin
untitled, Rebekka Marianne
you can be the cheese or you can be the hole, derek beaulieu
Lungs, Luke Mortenson
untitled, Kate Dubensky
Letter to Kevin Lovers, Keith McDonald
"in memoriam: antonin walpurga r.i.p.," Anthony Dawber
a tawny wanderer, Riel Hahn
untitled, Meghan Doraty
untitled, Andrea McDonald
illustration, Trystan Carter
untitled, Amy Edgar
untitled, Jeremy Stewart
untitled, Jeffrey Brian Dobson
an except from your biography, Matt Bohun
untitled, Jamie King
Wanted, Riley Nox Strother
safety pins for zippers, Brittany Bjorndal
Jumble, Julie Siemens
Kevin McPherson: A Promising Reference?, Charlotte Helston
untitled, Gary Barwin
untitled, Rae Kennedy
untitled, Jeff T. Johnson
untitled, Bestfriend
Discerning Professor Dachshund, Kristian Eckhoff
untitled, Jonathan Ball
untitled, Jim Barmby
untitled, Brodie Muskett
poems to be performed by kevin mcpherson eckhoff, Moez Surani
untitled, Claire Donato
untitled, Kyle John
untitled, Laurel Eckhoff McPherson

Acknowedgements

Mega-gratitudes to all of the self-as-others who helped to counterfeit this mere form of a book! Some debts have been made, and some have been paid—together, we put the ode in owed! Impassable shout-outs to too many impossible mentors and tormentors, friends and fiends.

Portions of this work have appeared in *LIT*, in the *Avant Canada Anthology* from no press, as a chapbook from above/ground press, and as the subject of an interview with Gary Barwin on *Jacket2*—much supra-radical thanks to those editor people! Hella thanks also to *usable hippos* for hosting instructions for the final cut on their web-outta-site.

And hearty chest bumps of gratefulness to Jayzel for believing in it with real-people blood-fire plasma!

Colophon

Maufactured as the first edition of
Their Biography: an organism of relationships
in the Spring of 2015 by BookThug

Distributed in Canada by
the Literary press Group www.lpg.ca
Distributed in the US by
Small Press Distribution www.spdbooks.org

Shop online at www.bookthug.ca

BOOK
PRODUCTION
WAR ECONOMY
STANDARD

Type + design by Jay MillAr
Copy edited by Ruth Zuchter